PIANO/VOCAL SELECTIONS

CHARLIE AND THE CHOCOLATE FACTORY
BROADWAY EDITION

ISBN 978-1-5400-1243-2

7777 W. BLUEMOUND RD. P.O. BOX 13819 MILWAUKEE, WI 53213

In Australia Contact:
Hal Leonard Australia Pty. Ltd.
4 Lentara Court
Cheltenham, Victoria, 3192 Australia
Email: ausadmin@halleonard.com.au

Visit Hal Leonard Online at
www.halleonard.com

WILLY WONKA! WILLY WONKA!

Music by MARC SHAIMAN
Lyrics by SCOTT WITTMAN
and MARC SHAIMAN

CHARLIE: How can a man who sells choc-'late not know all the his-t'ry? I

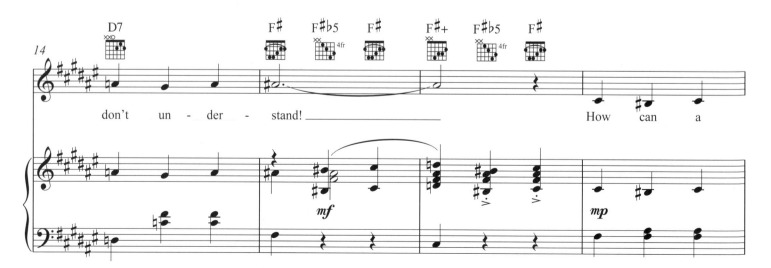

don't un-der-stand! _____ How can a

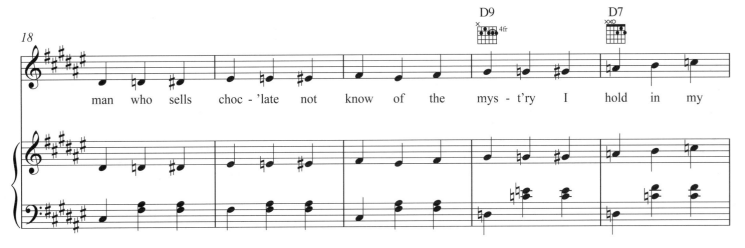

man who sells choc-'late not know of the mys-t'ry I hold in my

hand? _____ Wil - ly Wonk - a! Wil - ly Wonk - a!

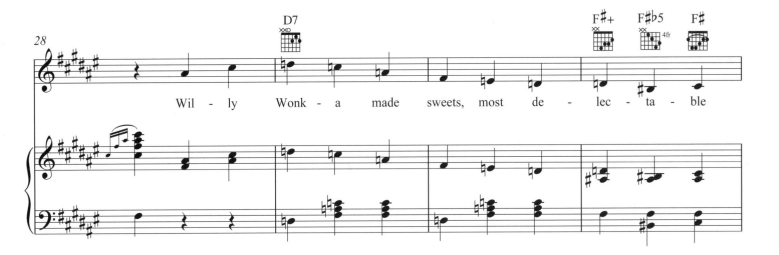

Wil - ly Wonk - a made sweets, most de - lec - ta - ble

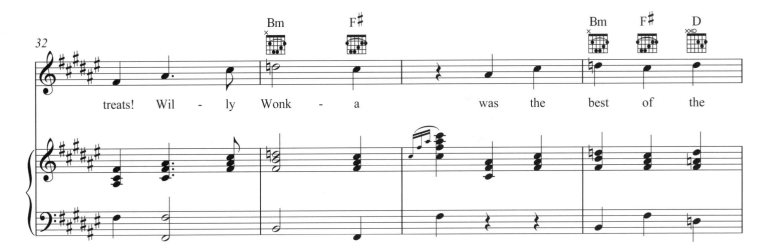

treats! Wil - ly Wonk - a was the best of the

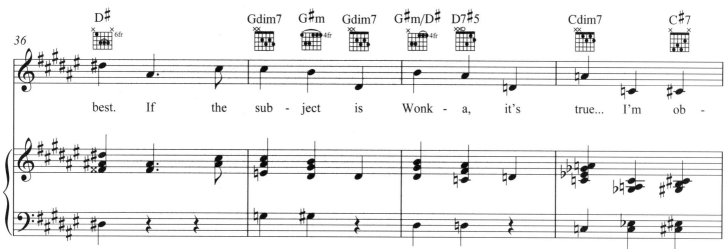

best. If the sub-ject is Wonk-a, it's true... I'm ob-

sessed! But

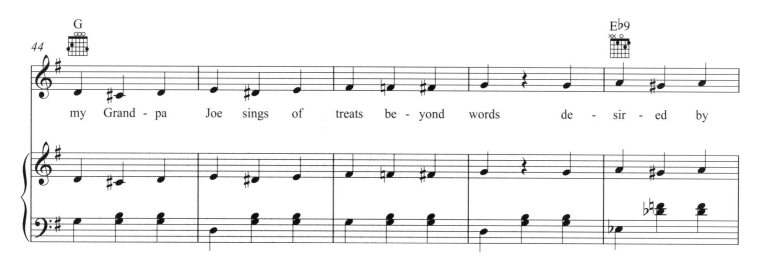

my Grand-pa Joe sings of treats be-yond words de-sir-ed by

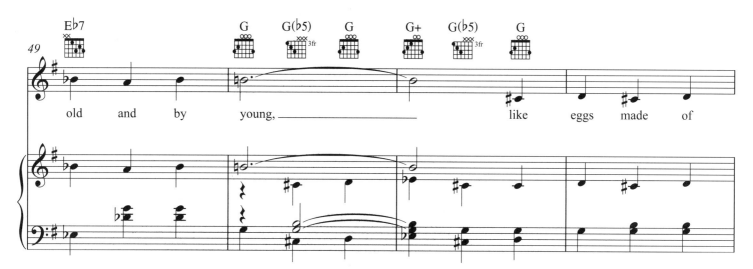

old and by young, _____ like eggs made of

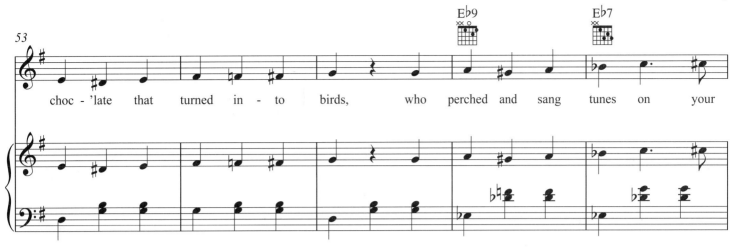

choc - 'late that turned in - to birds, who perched and sang tunes on your

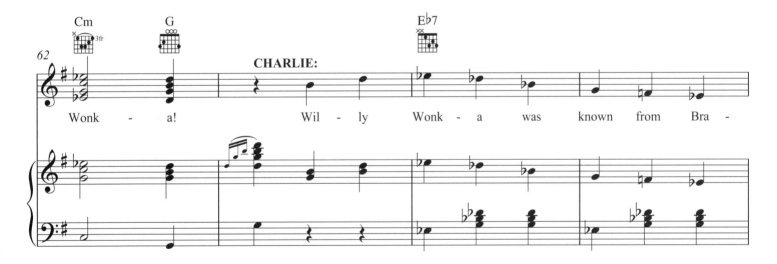

tongue! _____ Wil - ly Wonk - a! Wil - ly

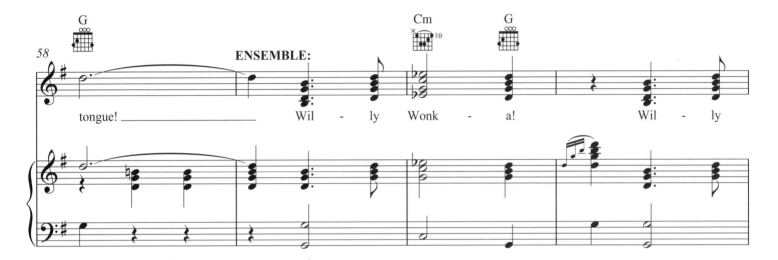

Wonk - a! Wil - ly Wonk - a was known from Bra -

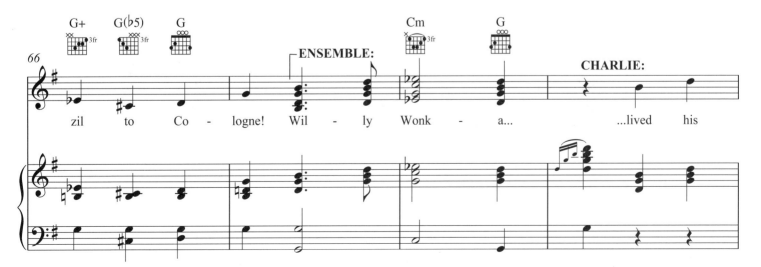

zil to Co - logne! Wil - ly Wonk - a... ...lived his

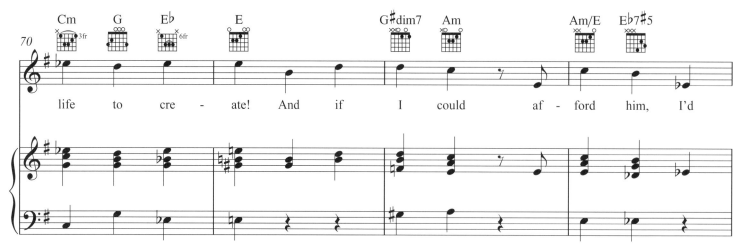

life to cre - ate! And if I could af - ford him, I'd

be o - ver - weight!

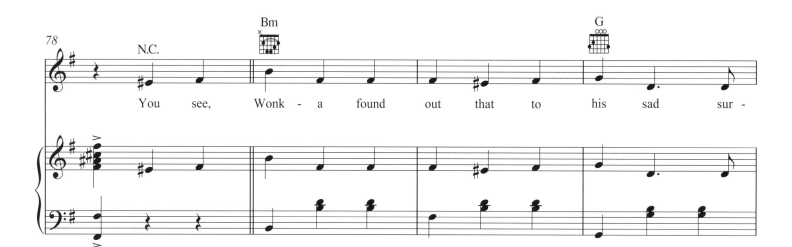

You see, Wonk - a found out that to his sad sur -

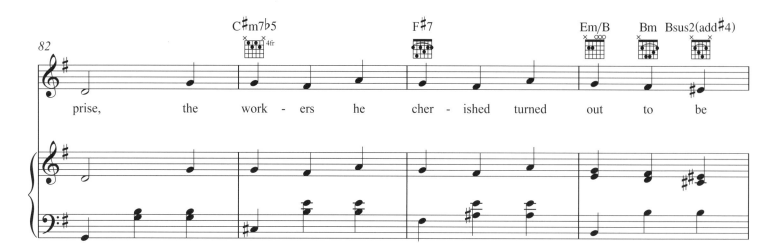

prise, the work - ers he cher - ished turned out to be

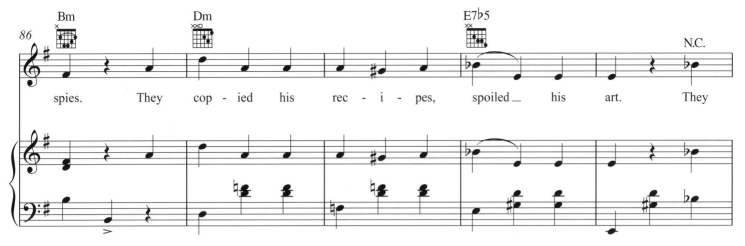

spies. They cop - ied his rec - i - pes, spoiled ___ his art. They

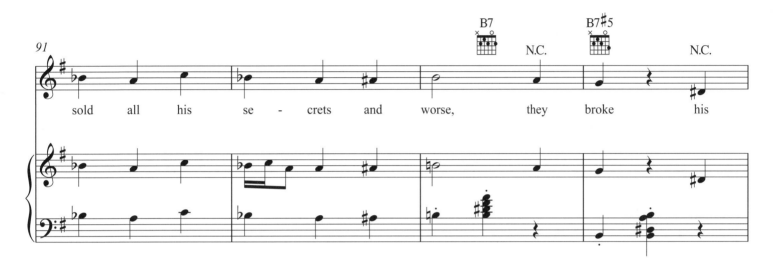

sold all his se - crets and worse, they broke his

heart. ___

And

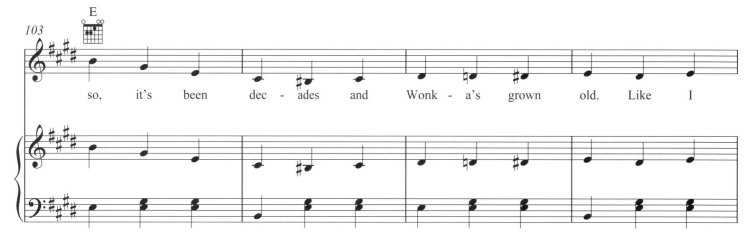

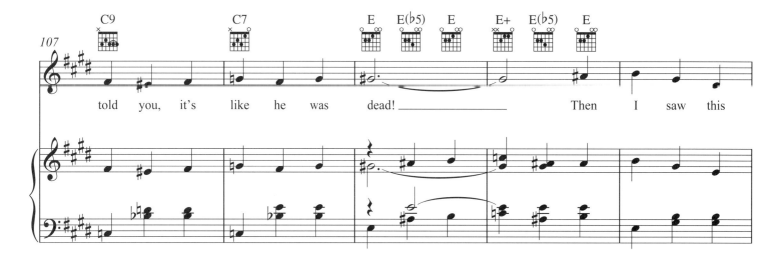

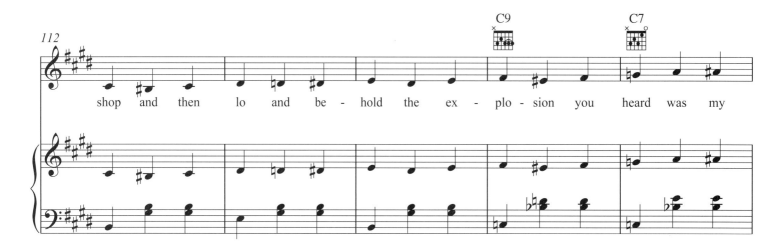

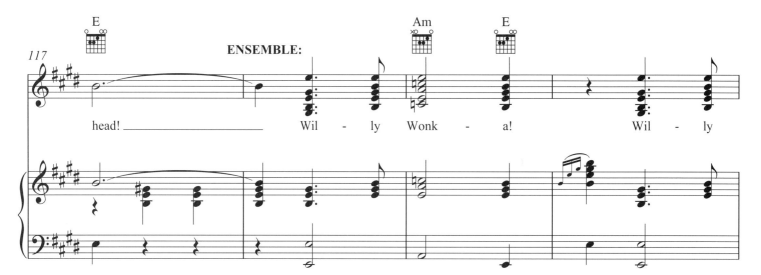

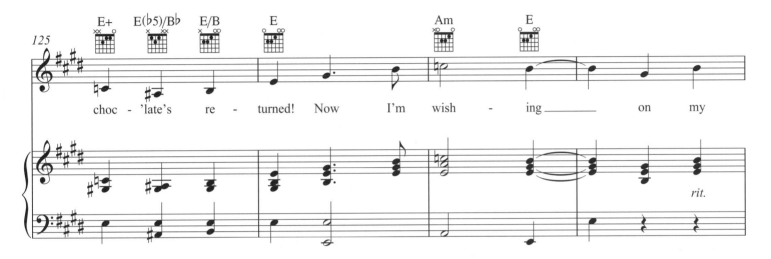

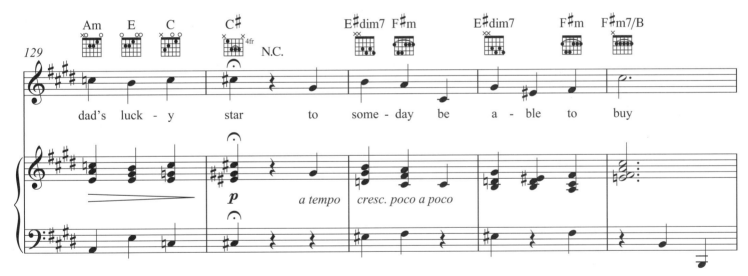

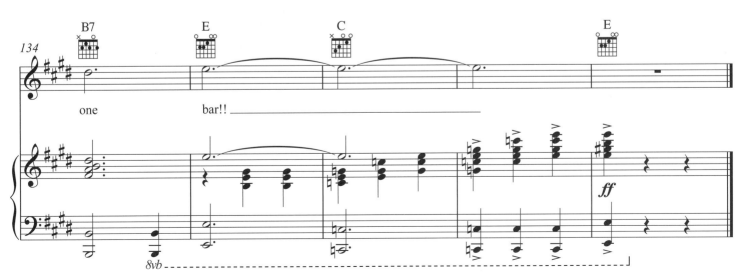

A LETTER FROM CHARLIE BUCKET

Music by MARC SHAIMAN
Lyrics by SCOTT WITTMAN
and MARC SHAIMAN

ask ya, "How'd ja do?" And, well, I'd like one Won-ka bar that

THE FAMILY:

I would share with you. Signed, Char-lie Buck-et. Good-

CHARLIE:

night, Char-lie Buck-et. Signed, Char-lie Buck-et, in-ven-tor.

rit.   *a tempo*

Freely

rit.

MORE OF HIM TO LOVE

Music by MARC SHAIMAN
Lyrics by SCOTT WITTMAN
and MARC SHAIMAN

seems just like a crumb, 'cause it turns out that des - sert was yet to
rolled, so round and sweet. _Und_ the first words that he ut - tered were...
AUGUSTUS: Let's

come! So we were eat! So _mit_
MRS. GLOOP:

stru - del he'd ca - noo - dle; how he loved my pret - zel pie. He ate the

whole kit and ca - boo - dle and grew wide as well as high. Though his

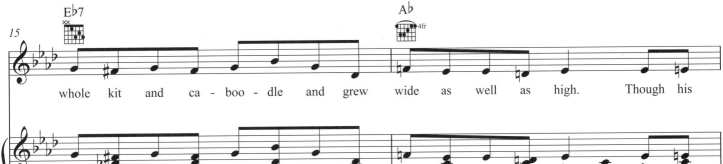

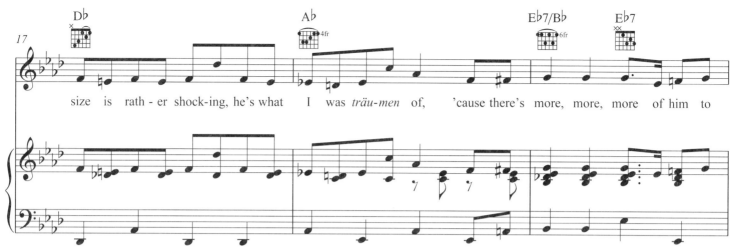

size is rath-er shock-ing, he's what I was *träu-men* of, 'cause there's more, more, more of him to

love. Like *mein*

AUGUSTUS:

Mut - ter und mein Va - ter, I en - joy a health - y meal. Yes, my

out - side's soft and flab - by, but my in - side's made of steel. We raise

pig - gies in *der* back - yard, then I eat them limb from limb. We don't

leave our poo - dles all a - lone with him.   So this

AUGUSTUS:

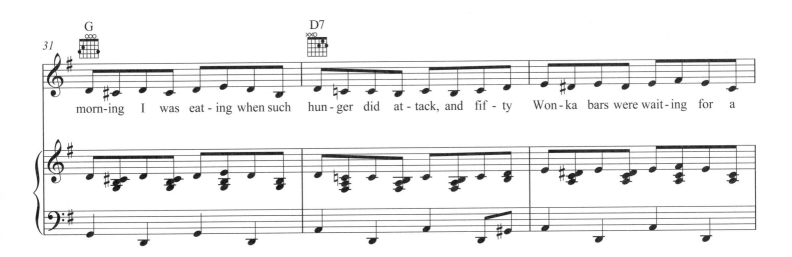

morn - ing I was eat - ing when such hun - ger did at - tack, and fif - ty Won - ka bars were wait - ing for a

nice mid - break - fast snack.   But the taste was kind - a dif - f'rent, like a

brat-wurst three days old, so I spit it out, and saw I had struck gold. Now, I'm the

per-fect tick-et win-ner, for on choc-o-late I did teethe. I'm ex-

cit-ed, but keep eat-ing 'cause I on-ly stop to breathe. And a life-time full of choc-'lates a *Ges-*

und-heit from a-bove. And there'll be more, more, more of me to love. **add MRS. GLOOP:** Yo-da-

lay-hee o-da-lay-hee, o-da-lay-hee, ____ tee-o lo-da lo-da lee.

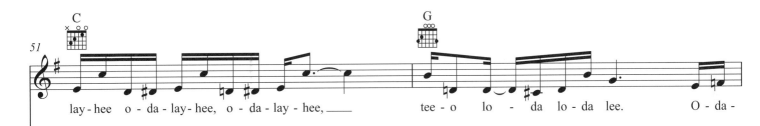

Tee-o lo-da lo-da lee. Tee-o lo-da lo-da lee. O-da-

lay-hee o-da-lay-hee, o-da-lay-hee, ____ tee-o lo-da lo-da lee. O-da-

lay-hee o-da-lay-hee, o-da-lay-hee, o-da-lay-hee, o-da-lay tee-o lo-da lo-da lee.

WHEN VERUCA SAYS

Music by MARC SHAIMAN
Lyrics by SCOTT WITTMAN
and MARC SHAIMAN

When Ve - ru - ca says, "More!" I
ru - ca says, "Out!" there's no

buy an - oth - er store. And when Ve - ru - ca says, "Now!" the
rea - son - a - ble doubt. And when Ve - ru - ca says, "Fetch!" there's

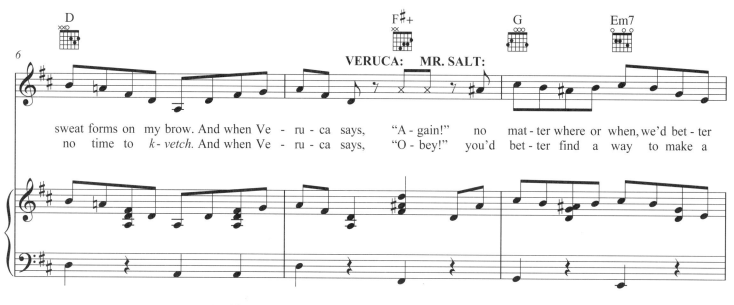

sweat forms on my brow. And when Ve - ru - ca says, "A - gain!" no mat - ter where or when, we'd bet - ter
no time to k - vetch. And when Ve - ru - ca says, "O - bey!" you'd bet - ter find a way to make a

THE QUEEN OF POP

Music by MARC SHAIMAN
Lyrics by SCOTT WITTMAN
and MARC SHAIMAN

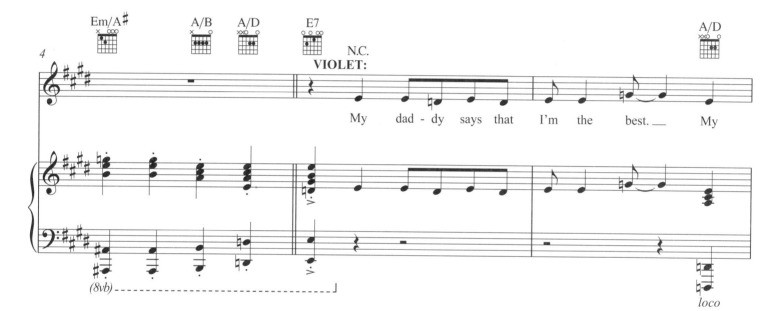

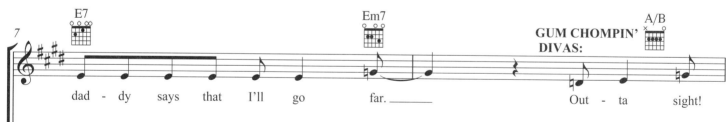

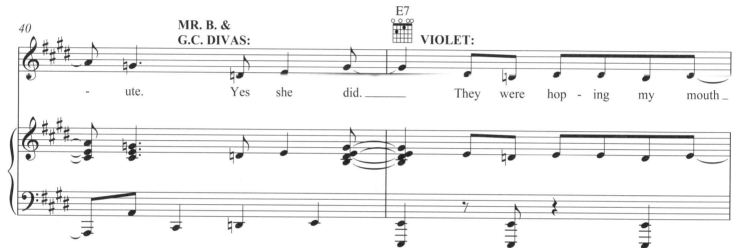

WHAT COULD POSSIBLY GO WRONG?

Music by MARC SHAIMAN
Lyrics by SCOTT WITTMAN
and MARC SHAIMAN

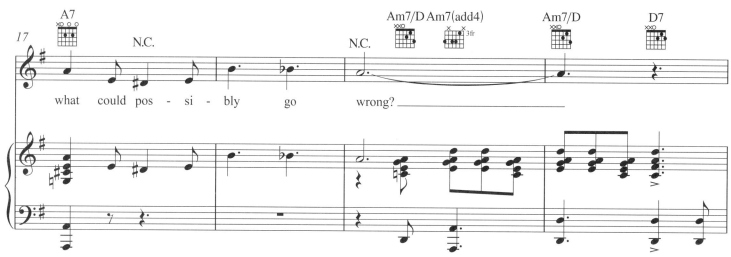

what could pos-si-bly go wrong? _____

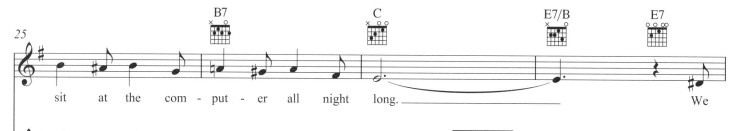

Here in the bos-om of A-mer-i-ca we

sit at the com-put-er all night long. _____ We

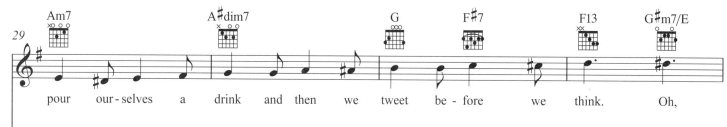

pour our-selves a drink and then we tweet be-fore we think. Oh,

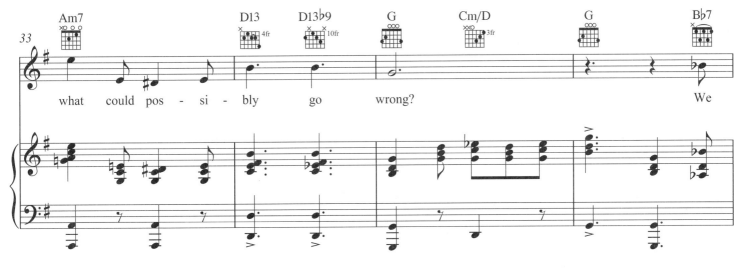

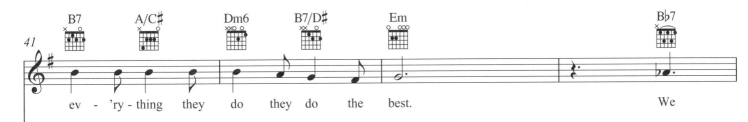

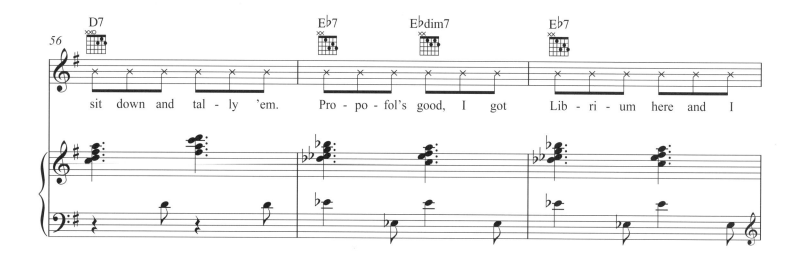

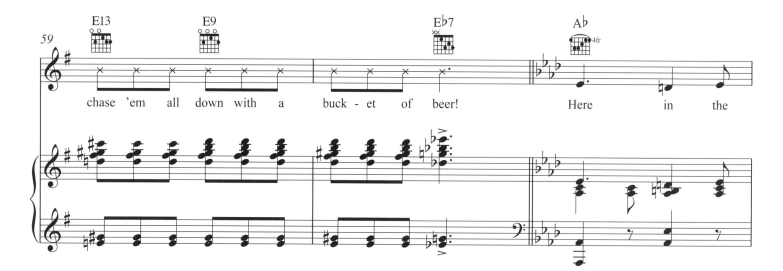

Lock her a - way! __ Mike Tea - vee is chang - ing up the U. S. A. __ I

hacked a Gold - en Tick - et; that's how I won. __ You got - ta break rules to get __

__ the job done. I don't need to go out - side to be what I'll be. __ Re -

al - i - ty is some - thing I can get from T - V. __ A - mer - i - ca, get read - y for my

cy - ber at - tack. ___ Mike Tea - vee is win - ning, there's

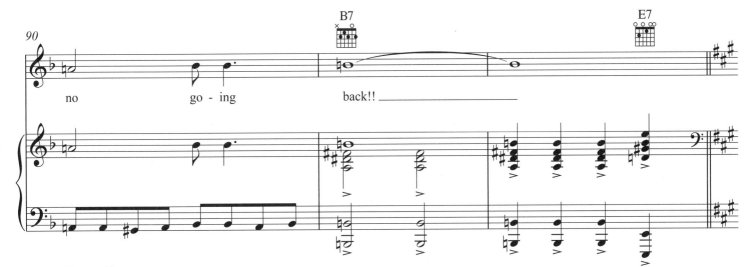

B7 E7

no go - ing back!! _____

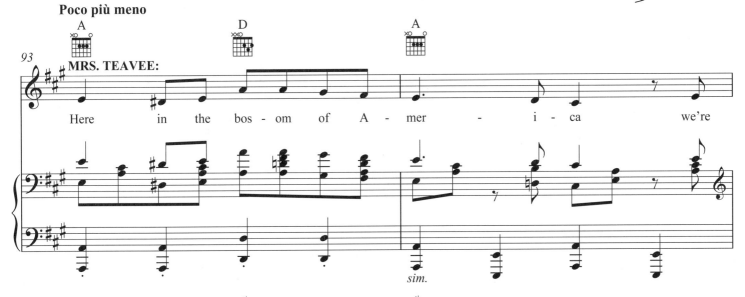

Poco più meno

A D A

MRS. TEAVEE:

Here in the bos - om of A - mer - i - ca we're

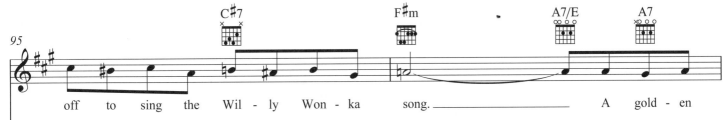

C#7 F#m A7/E A7

off to sing the Wil - ly Won - ka song. _____ A gold - en

IF YOUR FATHER WERE HERE

Music by MARC SHAIMAN
Lyrics by SCOTT WITTMAN
and MARC SHAIMAN

we can of - fer you _ are dreams in ev - 'ry size, so, close your eyes, _

_ Char - lie Buck - et, close your eyes... _

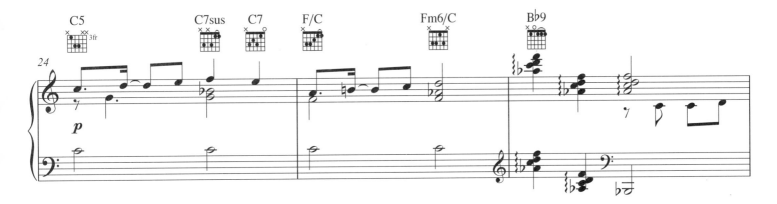

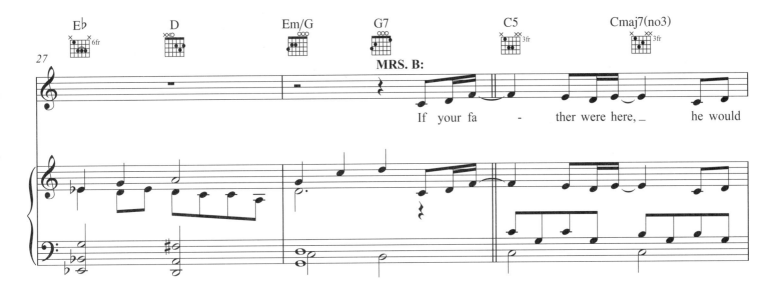

MRS. B:

If your fa - ther were here, _ he would

ban - ish the cold. ___ I can still feel his laugh - ter and I stop ___

___ feel - in' old. ___ As I'm watch - ing you grow, ___ inch by inch by inch by

Slower **Tempo I**

year, I would thank him if your fa - ther were here.

I'VE GOT A GOLDEN TICKET/ GRANDPA JOE

I'VE GOT A GOLDEN TICKET
Words and Music by LESLIE BRICUSSE
and ANTHONY NEWLEY

GRANDPA JOE
Music by MARC SHAIMAN
Lyrics by SCOTT WITTMAN
and MARC SHAIMAN

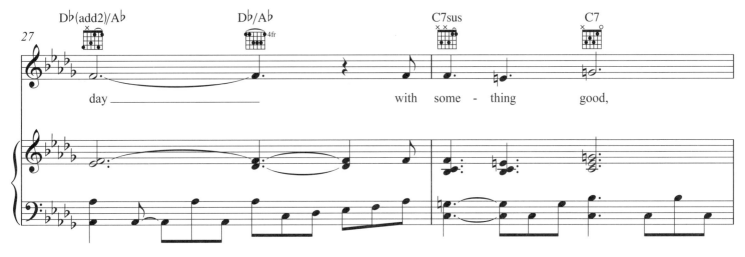

day _____ with some - thing good,

some - thing gold, some - thing spe - cial ___ that

I can hold! Grand - pa Joe, just

as you planned, ___ the fi - nal gold - en tick - et's in my

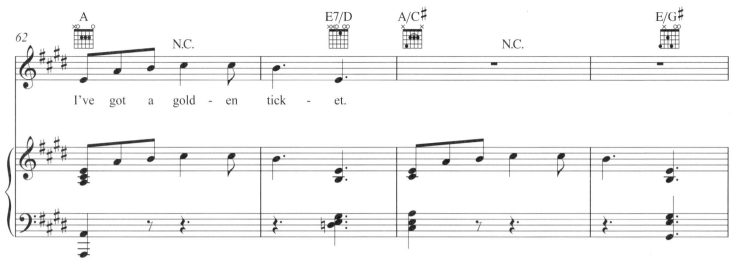

I've got a gold - en tick - et.

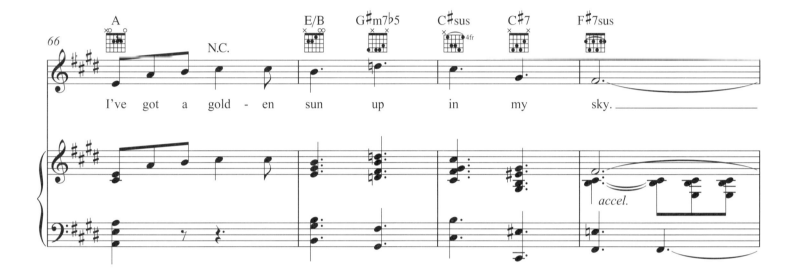

I've got a gold - en sun up in my sky. _____

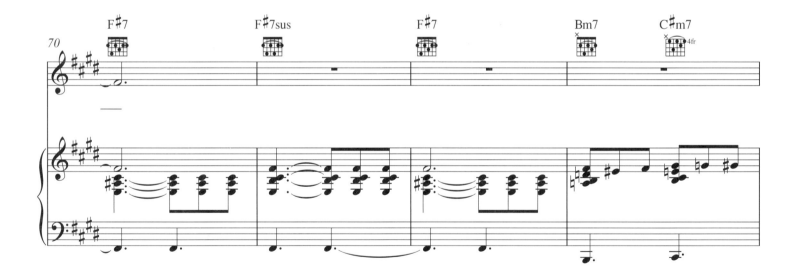

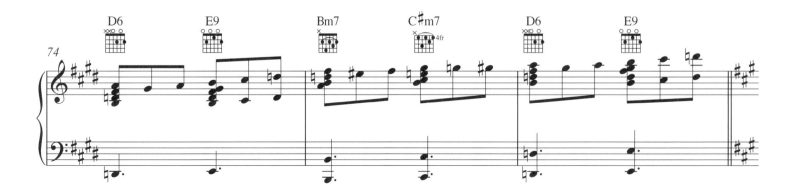

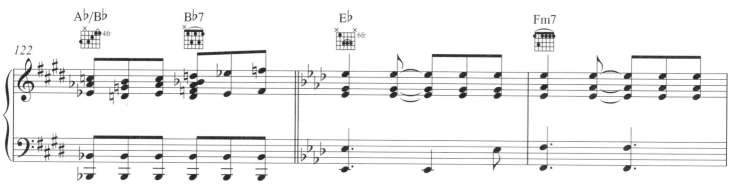

GEORGINA, GEORGE, JOSEPHINE,
MRS. BUCKET & CHARLIE:

We nev - er thought we'd see the day

when he would face the world and say, "Good morn - ing! _____

GRANDPA JOE:

____ look at the sun!"

IT MUST BE BELIEVED TO BE SEEN

Music by MARC SHAIMAN
Lyrics by SCOTT WITTMAN
and MARC SHAIMAN

be be - lieved _ to be seen. No mag - ic spells _ nor po -

- tions; for - swear _ leg - er - de - main! _ My

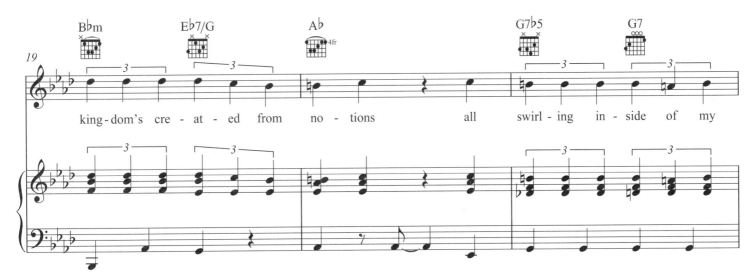

king - dom's cre - at - ed from no - tions all swirl - ing in - side of my

brain. Be - yond _ this door's _ a ban - quet of Won -

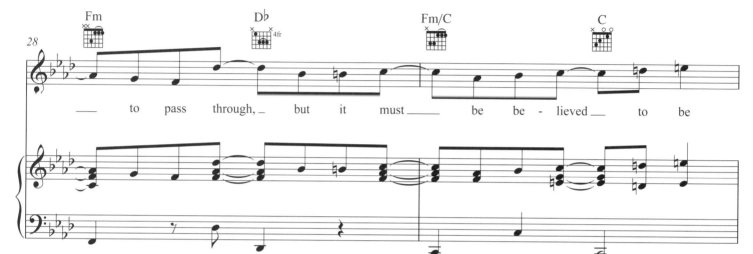

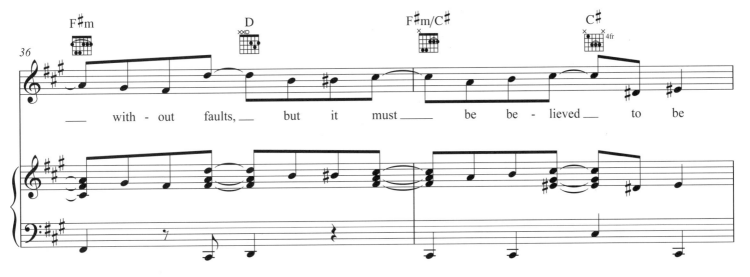

with - out faults, ___ but it must ___ be be - lieved ___ to be

seen. Be - yond ___ this door's ___ a puz - zle; you'll find ___

___ out what ___ I mean. ___ Be - yond ___ this gate ___ is the world ___

Misterioso e più mosso (straight 8ths)

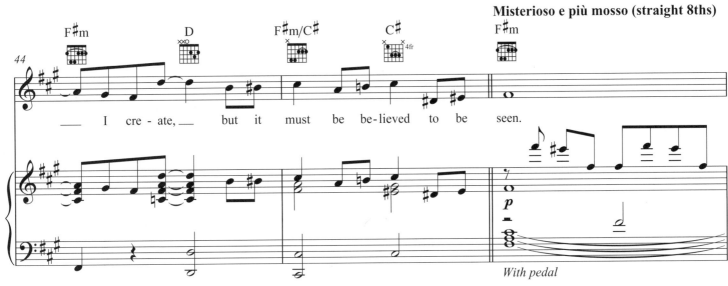

___ I cre - ate, ___ but it must be be - lieved to be seen.

With pedal

STRIKE THAT, REVERSE IT

Music by MARC SHAIMAN
Lyrics by SCOTT WITTMAN
and MARC SHAIMAN

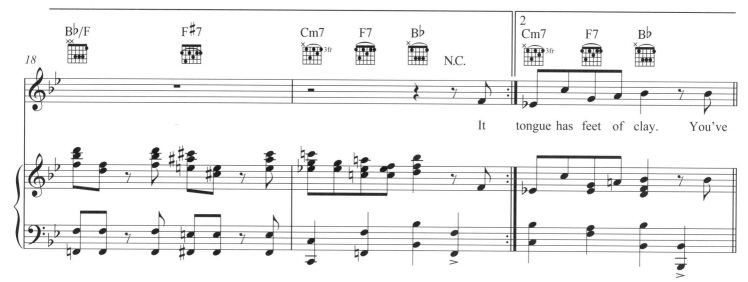

It tongue has feet of clay. You've

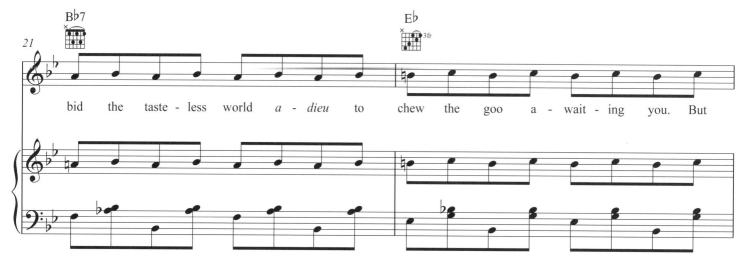

bid the taste-less world *a - dieu* to chew the goo a - wait-ing you. But

scur - ry, for the Won - ka clock keeps tick - ing. In -

side those doors, the floors are sweet. There's rugs and car - pets you can eat. And

No, strike that! Re - verse it! Let's get on with our day.

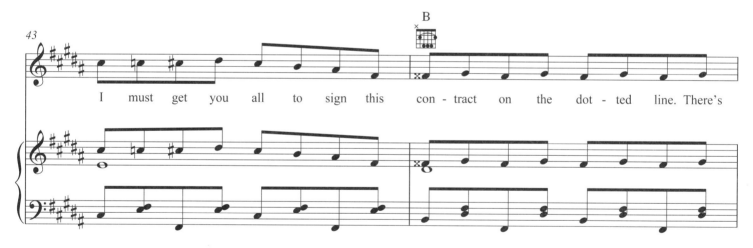

Faster (♩ = 170)

I'd love to lounge and lol - ly - gag and give each tongue the chance to wag, but

I must get you all to sign this con - tract on the dot - ted line. There's

no re - prise, the way time flies, to "dot the t's and cross the i's"...

PURE IMAGINATION

Words and Music by LESLIE BRICUSSE
and ANTHONY NEWLEY

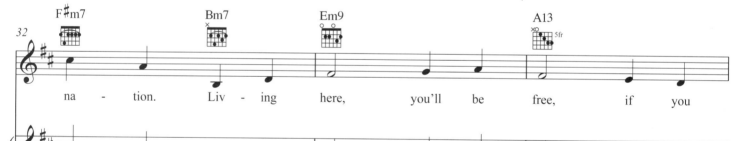

WHEN WILLY MET OOMPA

Music by MARC SHAIMAN
Lyrics by SCOTT WITTMAN
and MARC SHAIMAN

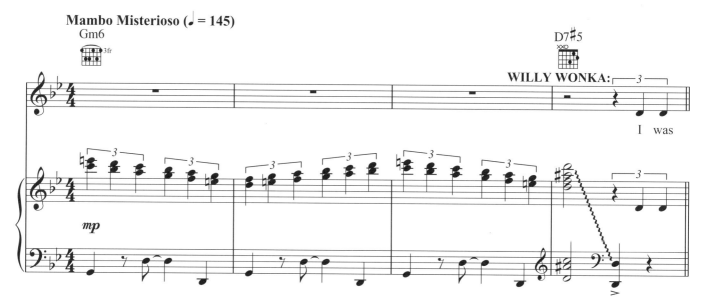

heav-en-ly choc-'late a-ro-ma. But the jun-gle was filled with Snozz-

wang-ers, Horn-swog-glers and wick-ed Whang-doo-dles, who would

make you their lunch as your bones they would crunch while they boil-ed your limbs for

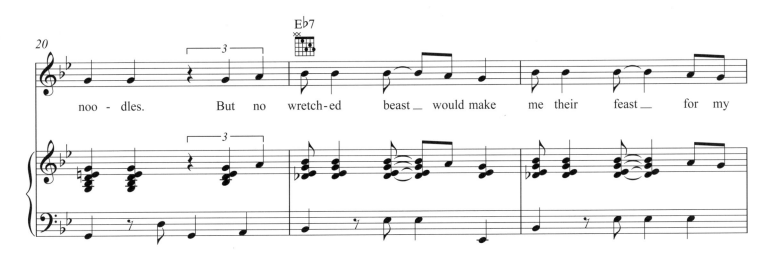

noo-dles. But no wretch-ed beast __ would make me their feast __ for my

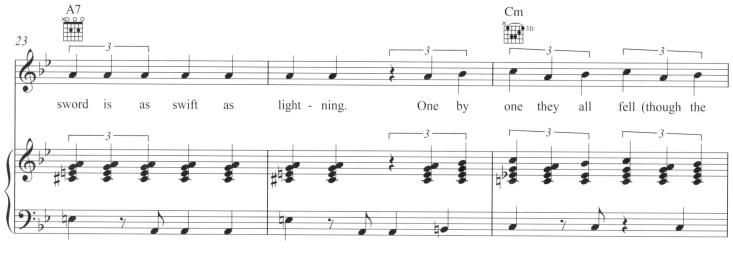

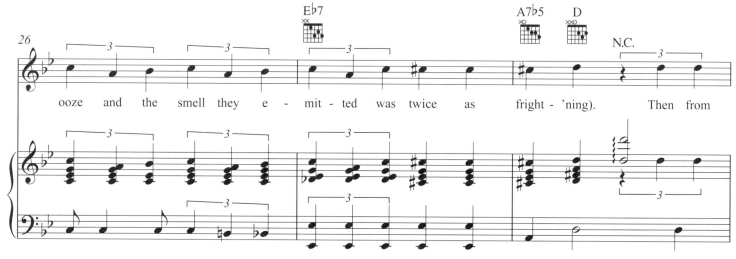

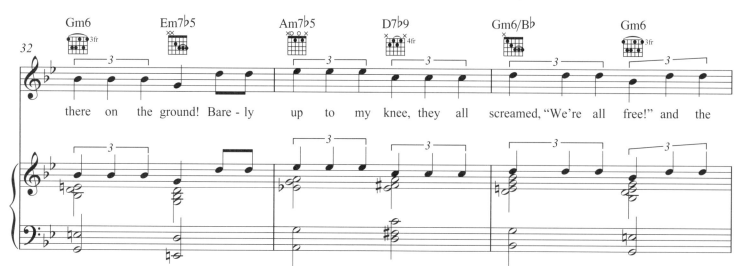

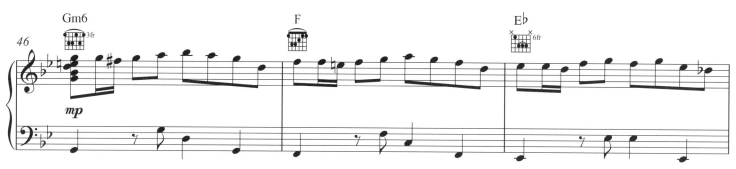

I said, "If you like this buf - fet, you will sim - ply

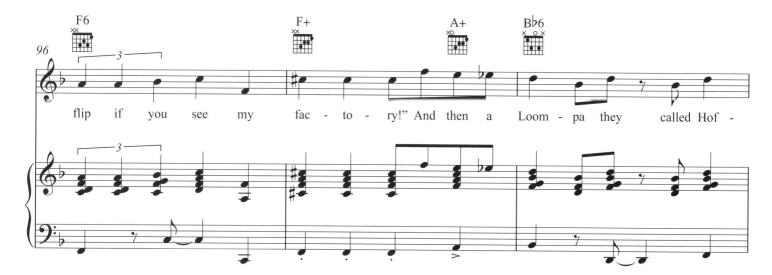

flip if you see my fac - to - ry!" And then a Loom - pa they called Hof -

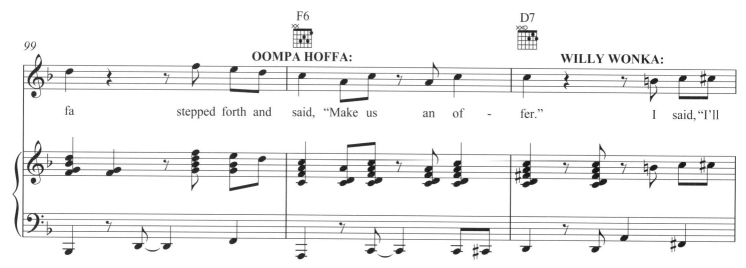

OOMPA HOFFA: **WILLY WONKA:**

fa   stepped forth and said, "Make us an of - fer."   I said, "I'll

OOMPA HOFFA:

pay you in beans if you man my ma - chines." He said, "I ain't no schnook, we want

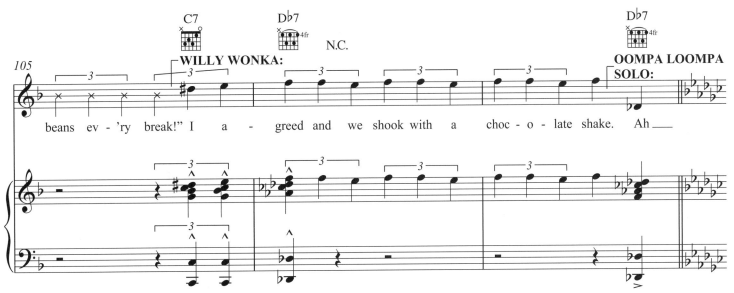

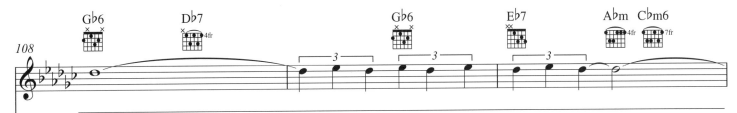

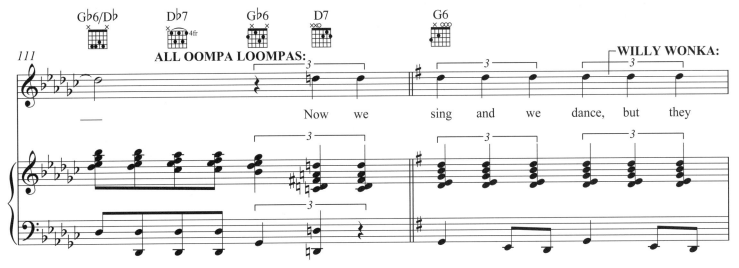

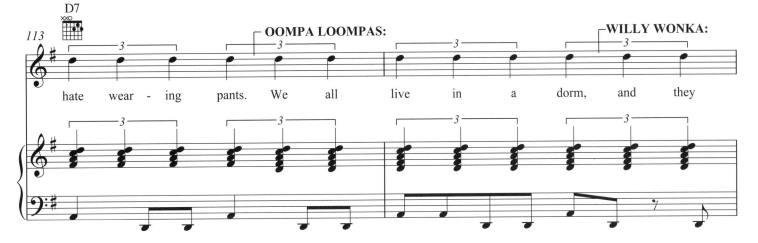

OOMPA LOOMPAS: ... **WILLY WONKA:**

love to per - form. Ev - 'ry wife is ex - ot - ic, though

that one's neu - rot - ic. The fun won't di - min - ish,

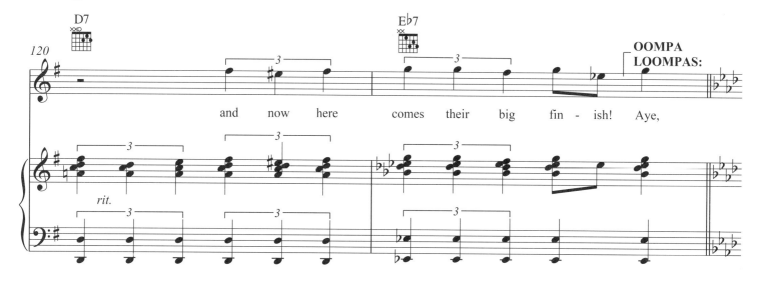

and now here comes their big fin - ish! Aye,

OOMPA LOOMPAS:

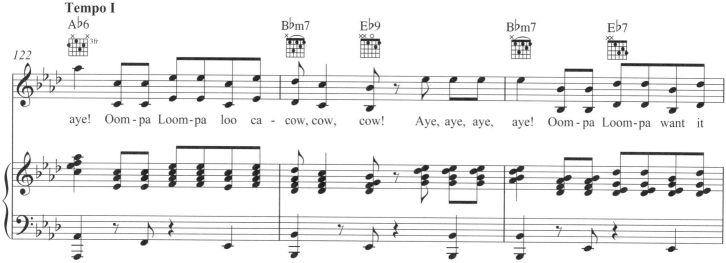

Tempo I

aye! Oom - pa Loom - pa loo ca - cow, cow, cow! Aye, aye, aye, aye! Oom - pa Loom - pa want it

THE VIEW FROM HERE

Music by MARC SHAIMAN
Lyrics by SCOTT WITTMAN
and MARC SHAIMAN

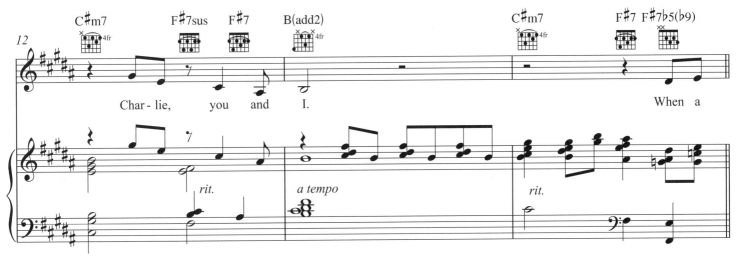

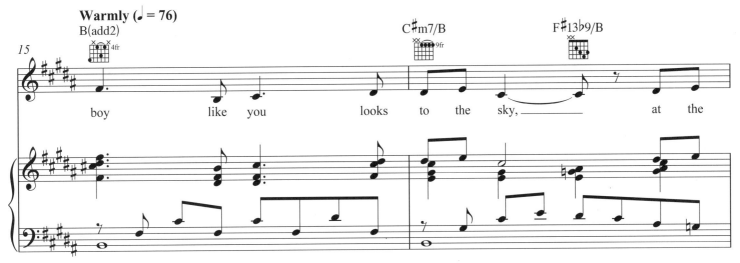

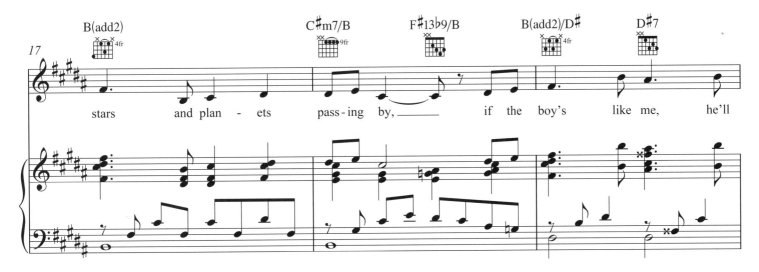

98

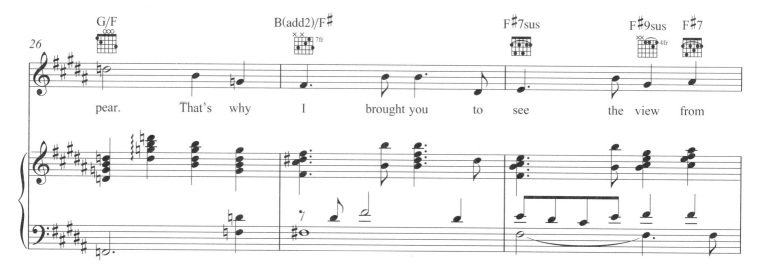

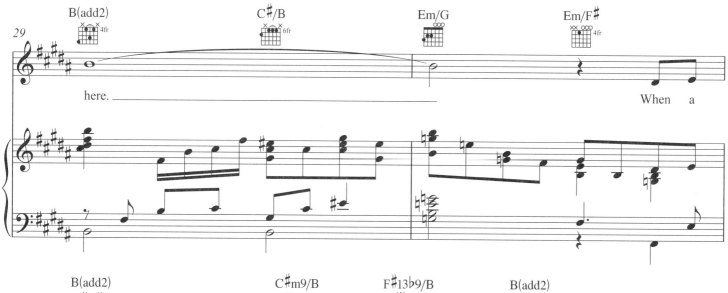

see the view from here._____ So you could

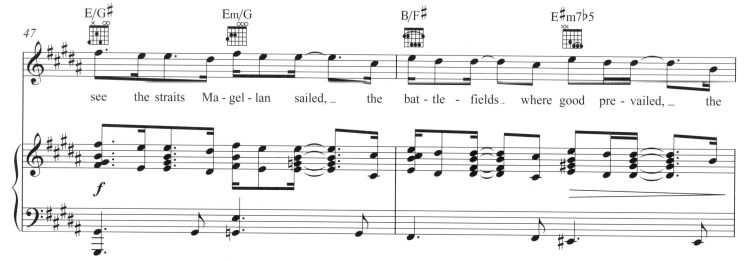

see the straits Ma-gel-lan sailed, _ the bat-tle-fields _ where good pre-vailed, _ the

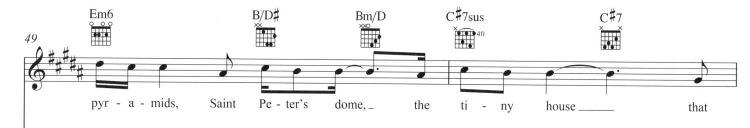

pyr-a-mids, Saint Pe-ter's dome, _ the ti-ny house_____ that

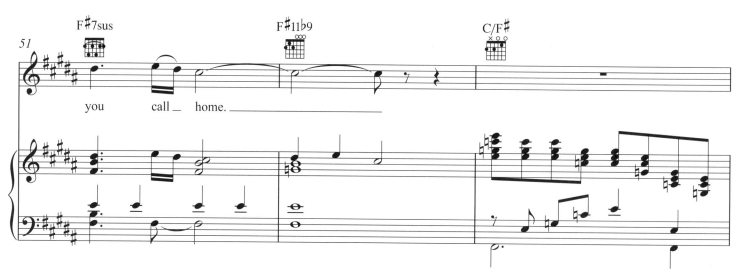

you call _ home._____

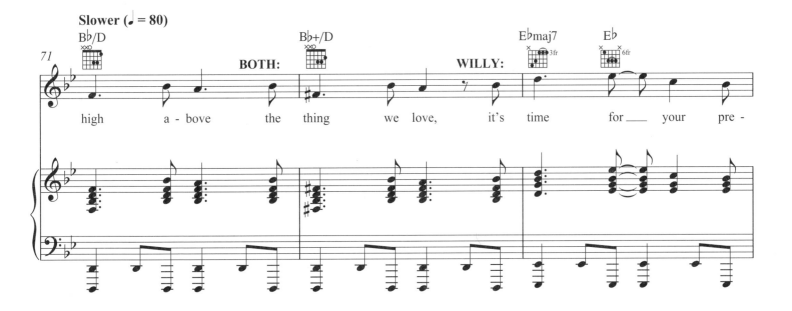